SIGNS OF
HEALTHY LOVE

About the pamphlet:
  Most of us are, have been, or will be involved in a signifi-
cant love relationship. When we know the signs of healthy
love, our chances of achieving fulfillment in our love for
another increase. This pamphlet outlines the characteristics of
mature, healthy love and suggests how to avoid dependent or
addictive relationships.

About the author:
  Brenda Schaeffer, M.A., is a psychotherapist and trainer of
therapists in Minneapolis, Minnesota. She is a certified
transactional analyst. Her model of therapy is integrative and
includes many disciplines. She has lectured internationally
and has authored several publications.

SIGNS OF
HEALTHY LOVE

BRENDA SCHAEFFER

First published March, 1986.

ISBN: 0-89486-374-6

Printed in the United States of America.

Editor's Note:
   Hazelden Educational Materials offers a variety of infor-
mation on chemical dependency and related areas. Our
publications do not necessarily represent Hazelden or its
programs, nor do they officially speak for any Twelve Step
organizaton.

INTRODUCTION

Viktor Frankl, who developed a school of existential psychiatry out of his own harrowing experiences in Auschwitz, has written of a revelation he experienced during his darkest days in a Nazi concentration camp: ". . . I saw the truth as it is set into song by so many poets, proclaimed as the final wisdom by so many thinkers — that love is the ultimate and highest goal to which man can aspire. The salvation of man is through love and in love. I understand how a man who has nothing left in this world still may know bliss . . . in the contemplation of his beloved. Love goes very far beyond the physical person of the beloved. It finds its deepest meaning in his spiritual being, his inner self."

Our goal in loving is not dependency on another, but *healthy belonging.* We experience most profoundly the meaningful inner self Frankl wrote of in our healthy love for each other. Addiction to another person is not true love. Love and addiction are separate entities that may come together for a time when one is mistaken for the other.

WHAT IS LOVE ADDICTION?

Stanton Peele, author of *Love and Addiction,** defines addiction as "an unstable state of being, marked by a compulsion to deny all that you are or have been in favor of some new and ecstatic experience." Addiction, Peele states, is "a malignant outgrowth of human inclinations." Words we often associate with addiction include obsessive, excessive, destructive, compulsive, habitual, attached, and dependent. And when you think about it, some of those words are also used to talk about love. Does this mean love is a habit we have to kick? No, not at all. Our purpose is to keep unhealthy addictive elements out of our love lives and bring healthy love in. Most love relationships are not either good or bad; rather they have elements of both.

---

*Available through Hazelden Educational Materials., order #6489.

1

Most of our habits and practices, which might have some elements of addiction, are not unhealthy. Many things we believe we need, we really *do* need for survival; and in moderation, these things are okay — food, shelter, stimulation, recognition, belonging.

I believe love addiction is our reliance on someone outside ourselves in an attempt to get our unmet needs fulfilled, to avoid fear or emotional pain, to solve problems, and to maintain our balance. *The paradox is that love addiction is an attempt to gain control of our lives, and in so doing, we lose control by giving personal power to someone other than ourselves.* It is often associated with feelings of "never having enough" or "not being enough." Love addiction is also a form of passivity in that we do not directly resolve our own problems but attempt to manipulate others so they will take care of us and thus take care of our problems.

If you recognize symptoms of unhealthy dependency in yourself and your relationship, you aren't alone. In our struggle to end our sense of isolation and irrelevancy, we often find ourselves snared in a web of neediness. Why bother to move from troublesome dependency to mature, fulfilling love? Isn't any love better than no love at all? There's a good answer to these questions. *Addictive love is limiting.* It limits our capacity for intimacy and our ability to truly love another as an equal. It limits our personal power and our freedom. It even limits our ability to feel content.

By knowing the signs of healthy love, we increase our chances of finding fulfillment in love. With mature love the individuals find it easy to know what they need and to reach out for it. Such lucky people accept their right to be loved; they are open, trusting, and undemanding.

CHARACTERISTICS OF HEALTHY BELONGING

We do need other people. We need to love and be loved in order to bloom to our fullest. As Erich Fromm said, "The affirmation of one's own life, happiness, growth, freedom, is rooted in one's capacity to love — in care, respect, responsibility, and knowledge."

We are the most highly-evolved species on the planet. We continue to evolve. In our evolution, there is a developing spiritual awareness that we are linked with other people in a very profound way. Each individual's uniqueness contributes to the greater whole of humankind.

Each of us is an individual energy system. If we think of ourselves this way, we realize we can choose to inhibit our energy, use it in destructive ways, or harness it for use in constructive ways. Even love can be viewed as a form of energy we suppress or exercise. Love is much more than a theoretical concept, and it makes sense to know more about *how* we love — whether it is dependent love aimed at ego enhancement and need fulfillment, or mature love that has evolved over time.

In knowing the qualities of healthy belonging, you can learn acceptance of yourself and others; and your chances of achieving fulfillment in love increase. We turn now to focus on the signs of healthy love. A fulfilling and mature love relationship has these qualities:

1. Allows for individuality
2. Experiences both oneness with and separateness from a lover
3. Brings out the best qualities in partners
4. Accepts endings
5. Experiences openness to change and exploration
6. Invites growth in the other
7. Experiences true intimacy
8. Feels the freedom to ask honestly for what is wanted
9. Experiences giving and receiving in the same way
10. Does not attempt to change or control the other
11. Encourages self-sufficiency of partners
12. Accepts limitations of self and partner
13. Does not crave unconditional love
14. Finds commitment acceptable
15. Has a high self-esteem

16. Trusts the memory of the beloved; enjoys solitude
17. Expresses feelings spontaneously
18. Welcomes closeness; risks vulnerability
19. Cares with detachment
20. Affirms equality of self and partner

Let's explore these characteristic signs of healthy love one by one.

Allows for Individuality

While addictive love causes us to feel we are being consumed, true love *allows for individuality*. A healthy relationship allows the lovers to change and grow in separate ways without one lover feeling threatened. Such freedom is possible because of the mature lover's respect and trust for a partner. Individual thoughts and feelings are accepted, not suppressed. Body and mind can remain relaxed when differences and conflicts arise, because differences are acceptable and resolution of conflict is considered a part of normal, everyday life. Even though we're partners, we don't feel we have to "take care" of each other's feelings. We are self-directed enough not to panic when our beloved is mentally preoccupied elsewhere.

Experiences Both Oneness With and Separateness From a Lover

Although mature lovers may describe their closeness as "oneness," they also have a clear sense of being separate individuals. That is, *oneness and separateness are both experienced and are not contradictory.* This allows for a state of euphoria denied addictive lovers, who are obsessed with the relationship at the expense of the self.

Netty was able to learn this truth and purge her obsessive feelings of dependency on her husband.

Netty had entered marriage counseling with her husband of fifteen years, Cliff, who recently had undergone successful treatment for chemical dependency. After many group sessions, Netty announced with joy that she was ready to leave therapy. She felt love for Cliff that she'd not experienced before, she said.

4

For years, Netty, who was haunted by low self-esteem and fear of rejection, had tried to make her husband love her in a fashion that matched her ideal of romance and marriage, insisting he make up for the losses she had experienced as a child. Not only had Cliff not responded, but Netty's unrealistic demands widened the rift between them. Netty's ideal — like that of many people who think of their illusions as "romantic" — assumed an almost suffocating dependency on Cliff.

In therapy, Netty had learned she could be whole by herself and that she did not *need* her husband. *Wanting* him was a very different — and much more gratifying — emotion. Netty now knew Cliff could not make up for what she had missed in her childhood. This realization eased much of her frustration, anger, and fear of rejection; and this, in turn, allowed her to relax mentally, emotionally, and physically. With less stress plaguing her, Netty was freer to explore her own talents and dreams. Netty gradually began to understand that self-love frees one to love others while allowing them their individuality.

Brings Out the Best Qualities in Partners

One rather subtle, but very visible and wonderful aspect of mature love, is that it *brings out the best in us*. In fact, it invites us to a higher quality of life, for it urges from our depths the highest human qualities: respect, patience, self-discipline, commitment, cooperation, generosity, and humility. Make no mistake — mature love isn't always easy, but in the final analysis, it feels right. Mature love is for grownups, and achieving it is part of the process of growing up.

Accepts Endings

Mature love *accepts endings*. The death of a relationship is inevitably painful, but mature people have enough respect for themselves and their partners to cope when it ends. Mature people know how to let go of an unsalvageable relationship, just as they are able to survive crises in a healthy one. Even in their grief, they do not doubt they will love again.

We can survive pain, though there's no denying the power it holds over us. I've witnessed strong, silent people crumbling into tears when they are sexually betrayed by a lover, even when they may themselves have cheated on their partner.

Upon learning his wife was having an affair, one man said to me, "I have never felt so much pain in all my life. I honestly don't know if I can live through it. The funny thing is, I never thought about love before all this happened. She was just there, being my wife and helper, raising the kids. God, I feel terrible. I never, ever want to go through this again."

The tragedy in his last sentence is that he was programming himself to never again be open to love. In order not to lose such vital openness, a wounded lover must transcend the natural tendency to react with anger, fear, and panic. We have the power to surmount pain and grief, and to once again forgive and love.

It sounds difficult, and it is. It takes one's spiritual strength to overcome the strong, self-destructive feelings of pain and anger. With time, mature people are able to accept reality — even when it hurts — and to move on to the next chapter in their lives. They face up to problems and sorrows in the most rational, healthy way even though it isn't easy.

Experiences Openness to Change and Exploration

It follows that *openness to change and exploration* is evident in a mature lover. Life is a series of changes, yet many people cling to the familiar, disregarding their inner desire to grow as an individual and in a relationship. Openness to change can be risky — even lead to breakups — but without it, a relationship will lose its vibrancy.

Often, one partner continues on a growth spiral while the other clings stubbornly to the familiar and seemingly safe. That may mean trouble. Let's look at the story of Grant and Barbara.

Grant and Barbara met and fell in love when they were philosophy students in college. They were alive with the

6

excitement of discovering and sharing new ideas and experiences. After they married, their lives slowly began to change — and then, suddenly, everything came to a standstill. Grant worked outside the home; Barbara was a homemaker. Their upper-middle-class lifestyle, so different from their college ideals, featured a hectic social life and a quest for material possessions. Grant embraced his role as provider, loyal company man, and consumer. Barbara acted as faithful companion and supporter of her husband's career.

They had been married for about twelve years when boredom and restlessness began to drive a wedge between them. Barbara, approaching middle age, entered graduate school and once again began to be moved by new ideas and experiences. She was eager to share it all with Grant, but to her bewilderment, he resisted her and belittled her schoolwork. Frightened, Barbara ceased talking to him about her experiences. Meanwhile, Grant had extramarital affairs and began to drink too much. It was clear they had drifted apart. Their relationship was devoid of warmth and excitement. At that point, recognizing that their marriage was in peril, they sought counseling.

At first, Grant and Barbara saw the problem as one of communication, but they found it was much more profound. Because they had neglected individual growth in favor of intense social involvement and competition for business and status, their spiritual sides had stagnated. They suffered from the strong but vague sense that *something was missing*. The results were Barbara's very real excitement when she began once again to nurture her creative side and Grant's frustrated search for stimulation and excitement in casual sex and frequent drunkenness.

Without openness to change and exploration, a relationship is like a body that is never exercised — it loses flexibility and power; it weakens and may even die.

Invites Growth in the Other

Not only do mature people recognize that change is necessary, they know true love *urges and encourages growth in the other,* including the development of other important relationships without feelings of jealousy.

I spoke recently with a male friend who is very dear to me. At that moment, he was my most important friend and I was his. Though we knew we both had other vital friendships, no jealousy came between us. We spoke about how this might change if we were lovers. We concluded, somewhat puzzled, that often when sex is involved, other vital friendships do give rise to jealousy. Though there may be little rational reason for jealousy, it is an enormous force in our emotional and biological makeup. Jealousy is deeply rooted in our biology — perhaps the offspring of our primal urges toward procreation and protection — and it is also a learned social value. Jealousy is a natural emotion, but if we allow it to control us, we may cut off our own growth and that of our partner.

Personal development doesn't end at age eighteen; it continues until death. At mid-life, we are confronted with a choice: stagnation or personal self-discovery that may lead to a renewed growth. It's a time when many people feel confused and challenged. Because many people fear change, they may choose to stagnate intellectually and emotionally, and their other relationships suffer as a result.

Experiences True Intimacy

Because mature lovers are not held prisoner by private fears and inhibitions carried from childhood, their relationships feature *true, intense intimacy.* Fear of love's risks inhibits intimacy; trust and the willingness to take risks invite it. True love seems contradictory: those who are self-contained and independent are better able to deeply, tenderly love another. Because their love is not obsessive or *dependent,* they are free to be *inter*dependent, complementing each other.

That is, those who are *free* as individuals are also *free to love* as part of a healthy relationship. It may look like a paradox, but if you think about it, it's not.

Feels the Freedom to Ask Honestly for What Is Wanted

True love also features *freedom to ask and to receive,* as well as a willingness to accept no for an answer at times. It can't be stressed enough that the ability to be honest — to say no when one means no — is crucial in a relationship. In fact, one's yes cannot be trusted until one has also demonstrated the ability to say no. One crucial way I determine a formerly dependent client's readiness to leave therapy is his or her ability to reach out to others, to ask clearly for what is needed, and to receive help from others. It's also crucial that people be able to let go of their desire for things that cannot realistically be gotten.

Couples I work with frequently expect others to mind-read. They often say to each other: "You've lived with me long enough. You should know what I need by now!" That's a mistake. At times your partner *does* know what you need; at other times he or she can read you correctly, or may simply guess correctly. But most often it's crucial to negotiate, to talk about feelings and needs, for most of us are not mind readers. Even love does not make us clairvoyant!

With the help of therapy, Joan, a very hesitant, quiet woman of 35, had accomplished many new things. One was a new ability to talk honestly about what she was feeling and to directly ask her partner, Clark, for what she wanted, instead of expecting him to guess. One day she came to me feeling very sad and angry. "I did everything I was supposed to," she said. "I wanted Clark to do something for me and I asked him in a clear, gentle way. Do you know what he said? He said no! He refused me."

Joan had done the right things, but she'd made a common mistake: she thought if she asked in the right way, she'd get what she wanted. Although it's true we most often get what we want when we ask in a direct fashion, it's important to ask the right person at the right time, and even then accept that the person might not be in a position to give. Joan hadn't done that.

People often get into trouble when they *expect* to get what they need or want. Needing and wanting something is natural, but expecting or demanding to receive it only sets us up for disappointment.

This is true of love itself, for often we expect people to fit our ideal of love expression. One person in a relationship may enjoy running errands for the other, while the other may be more sentimental and give flowers, cards, and gifts. If they're both perceptive and mature, they'll know that the method of giving is unique to the giver, and many forms of love expression will be welcome. True lovers appreciate, even savor, such differences.

Experiences Giving and Receiving in the Same Way

Nonegocentric love *experiences giving and receiving similarly.* Pleasure obtained in giving to the beloved is as intense as that gained in receiving from him or her. When one has made the marvelous leap from dependency to freer love, one can give more easily and with fewer expectations. Most people give to please; by so pleasing, they hope to receive in return. When this fails, they may get angry and say, "Well, forget you! I've given and given and it didn't do any good!"

Anger and frustration often mark a turning point for a giver who gives to get. At this point the person may quit such ego-centered giving in frustration and begin to be more honest with his or her lover.

A client's spouse once called me and said, "I don't know about this therapy. My wife is driving me up a wall. She's angry all the time and refuses to do a thing for me." I said, "It's only a phase, and someday you'll know what I mean."

Weeks later, he called me to say: "You were right. She's back to her old self." In truth, the woman, who had been a "giver-to-get," *wasn't* back to her old self; she was very different. She was learning to give to her husband, to do things that pleased him, *not* because she expected anything in return, but because she truly loved him and was learning to experience the joy of giving for its own sake. Her anger and frustration over the failure of "giving-to-get" had been a natural phase — one in which some relationships collapse.

Does Not Attempt to Change or Control the Other

Mature love *accepts the self and others as they are.* One lover does not try to change or control the other. This does not assume the partners like everything about themselves or the other, but they are able to put dislikes into perspective. That is, the best romances are based on *realism.*

Though it may sound simple enough, one of the most difficult parts of love is learning to accept ourselves and others as we are. Life and relationships are filled with choices for us to make. If we choose to be with someone, accepting this person as is, that is real love. Attempting to change another person is a symptom of unhealthy dependency. And as anyone who has ever tried to change a lover knows, it never works. Never. Many a relationship has sunk against that reef of grief!

Encourages Self-Sufficiency of Partners

Mature love assumes *self-sufficiency in the partners.* Erich Fromm writes: "The most important step is to learn to be alone with oneself without reading, listening to the radio, smoking, or drinking. . . . This ability is precisely a condition for the ability to love." Mature love occurs when we realize we are substantial alone, that we no longer need another as we needed others in infancy and childhood. We have qualities within us that make us complete. In a healthy relationship, both individuals have a sense of self-esteem and well-being. They trust themselves and others; on a scale of zero to ten, they love themselves unconditionally — a ten! — without guilt. I believe we all have what it takes to love and respect ourselves that much.

Accepts Limitations of Self and Partner

True love involves a *realistic appraisal of our limitations.* Especially in love, it is crucial that we adjust our beliefs to what is real rather than trying to twist reality to fit what we want to believe. It may seem odd that in order to grow, we need to accept our limits. But mature love can solve problems *within* our limits.

Does Not Crave Unconditional Love

In a good love relationship, we *no longer crave unconditional love from our lover.* The reality is that the only time we needed that kind of care was in the first eighteen months of our lives; we no longer need it from others *because we can grant it to ourselves.* The marvelous paradox is that when we cease our search for unconditional love, we are often surprised to find someone loving us just that way.

Finds Commitment Acceptable

In dependent love, commitment often is experienced as a "loss of self." In mature love, the opposite is true; *self-esteem is enhanced.* Commitment is experienced as expanding ourselves; we go beyond narcissistic self-gratification to share with, give to, and even sacrifice for our beloved. Commitment accepts, without resistance, the importance and value of the other person in one's life. There is a genuine concern for the commitment to the well-being of the other person. Each of us consider how our actions will affect the relationship. We recognize that independence is not always doing "what I want when I want it," but rather taking responsibility for our lives in ways *least* hurtful to ourselves and others. Autonomy includes boundaries and limits, and mature lovers *mutually define* these boundaries to enhance their commitment. Our commitment expresses our deepest values and transcends our fears.

> *"If I do my thing, and you do your thing*
> *And we don't live up to each other's expectations*
> *We might live, but the world will not survive.*
> *You are you, and I am I together, not by chance.*
> *Joining hands, we will find each other beautiful*
> *If not, we can't be helped."*
>
> — *Claude Steiner*

Has a High Self-Esteem

How much do you love yourself? In mature love, both individuals have a high sense of self-esteem and well-being. So often in dependent relationships, individual self-esteem will ebb and flow, depending upon the response of our relationship partner. In healthy belonging to each other, we trust in ourselves, and our self-esteem is not shaken by disapproval or discord.

I recall a relationship where I was asked to put the other person on a pedestal. He was saying, "I need you to look up to me so I can feel good about myself." While you and I can affirm another's worth and goodness, we cannot give others the self-esteem they lack. My response to my friend was direct: "Putting you up on a pedestal would be a lie. We are equals. I will not do so." The relationship ended, and he continued his search for a partner willing to revere him.

Sometimes others may put *you* on a pedestal, and there may be a temptation to stay there and enjoy the view. This is a very dangerous place . . . for what goes up, eventually comes down! Mature love is not a place for inflated egos either. I once heard humility defined as a "gentle acceptance of oneself." Mature lovers seem to express this quiet self-confidence alone and with each other.

Trusts the Memory of the Beloved; Enjoys Solitude

A crucial indicator of true love is our *ability to trust our memory of our absent lover* so we can accept and enjoy our time alone. Although we may want to be with our absent lover, we are confident he or she eventually will return. In the meantime, memories of good feelings are enough to satisfy us. Mature love assumes the individuals experienced sufficient response to childhood needs, so they find it easy to know what they need and to reach out for it; responses to those needs have been consistent enough so internal assurance blossoms. Such lucky people accept their right to be loved; they are open, trusting, and undemanding.

13

Expresses Feeling Spontaneously

In addictive, dependent love relationships, partners keep replaying old dramatic scenes leading to "favorite" bad feelings they haven't expressed such as confusion, anger, guilt, or shame. In a healthy relationship lovers spontaneously express *feelings that are based on what's actually happening*. Feelings are expressed, rather than suppressed, in nonabusive ways when they arise. Feelings expressed won't explode later at inappropriate times or implode, causing much physical and mental pain. Stored-up frustration and anger will come out sometime — you can be sure of it.

Welcomes Closeness; Risks Vulnerability

Mature lovers welcome the closeness of intimacy and risk being vulnerable. They have faced the reality of their aloneness and know the joys of sharing. They risk the vulnerability of sharing feelings, thoughts, dreams, play, affection, and sex. Partners can experience the being of each other. They know their closeness allows for individual differences, and the lovers see themselves as unique and different from each other. Their relationship complements and coexists with their individual freedom. The partners are confident their feelings will be respected and don't need to cut off from each other to protect themselves.

Cares with Detachment

Maturity brings with it the knowledge that we can care, listen, and respond to a lover's feelings, but we cannot "fix" or remove his or her ill feelings. Therefore, a *sense of caring detachment* is a healthy sign in a relationship. The partners say, "I care what you feel and I'm here for you," and not "Let me feel your pain for you."

When they first sought counseling Lea was terribly depressed and John, her husband, felt guilty about it. "I can't seem to spring her from this depression, and I've done everything I can think of," he said. "How am I supposed to feel good when she's so damn blue?" Secretly he felt a failure as a man and husband. He believed men are to be heroes, saviors of sad heroines.

John and Lea both had to learn that Lea was responsible for her own depression. While John could be understanding and sympathetic, he couldn't conquer it for her. In fact, John would find Lea's state of mind less depressing to himself if he felt less responsible for it. John was relieved when he realized this. Meanwhile, Lea was able to feel less guilty when John quit blaming himself for her depression, and thus she was more readily able to explore its underlying causes. John, less anxious, now offered more support. By letting go, they gave their relationship a chance to grow in strength and character.

Affirms Equality of Self and Partner

Finally, mature love *affirms the personal power of both lovers*. In true love, the lovers recognize each other as equals; they are not caught up in psychological games and "one-upmanship." When two people are content and free as individuals, their power springs from self-confidence, self-love, and a willingness to give to each other.

HEALTHY BELONGING

Mature lovers have conquered the question, "Who am I?" They have a sense of self-identity, self-esteem, and the knowledge that "I am enough alone." They know what they need and want, what is important, and what is not. In a healthy relationship the partners can appreciate their own individual talents, interests, creative potential, and pursuits. They have a sense of healthy detachment and an awareness that each is capable of intimacy and love. Though the partners see themselves as unique and different from one another, they know their closeness allows for individual differences, that the relationship complements and coexists with individual freedom. Giving is spontaneous; there is emotional and spiritual bonding. Commitment is characterized by desire, not only to give to the other, but to serve the other without expecting something in return. The partners realistically allow for faults, failures, and disappointments. And there is equality.

The lovers know they no longer need people to survive as they once did in childhood, that life is harsh at times, unfair at times and, yet, continues to be good. They sing themselves to sleep at night and wake up refreshed in the morning!

The mature love relationship serves as our springboard for the extension of our energy and interest out into the world. Since trust pervades the healthy relationship, we need not be with our lover to feel energetic or nourished. The love we experience expands from an exclusive relationship to universal love that reinforces the belief that love does, indeed, make the world go 'round.

Love one another but make not a bond of love:
Let it rather be a moving sea between the shores of your
souls.
Fill each other's cup but drink not from one cup.
Give one another of your bread but eat not from the same
loaf.
Sing and dance together and be joyous, but let each one of
you be alone,
Even as the strings of a lute are alone though they quiver with
the same music.
Give your hearts, but not into each other's keeping.
For only the hand of Life can contain your hearts.
And stand together yet not too near together:
For the pillars of the temple stand apart,
And the oak tree and the cypress grow not in each other's
shadow.

— *from* The Prophet
by Kahlil Gibran